TO:

....

FROM:

....

Gobi

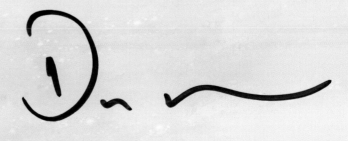

A LITTLE DOG
WITH A BIG HEART

Gobi

Dion Leonard

ILLUSTRATED BY LISA MANUZAK

Gobi

© 2017 Dion Leonard

All rights reserved. No portion of this book may be reproduced, stored in a retrieval system, or transmitted in any form or by any means—electronic, mechanical, photocopy, recording, scanning, or other—except for brief quotations in critical reviews or articles, without the prior written permission of the publisher.

Published in Nashville, Tennessee, by Tommy Nelson. Tommy Nelson is an imprint of Thomas Nelson. Thomas Nelson is a registered trademark of HarperCollins Christian Publishing, Inc.

Illustrated by Lisa Manuzak

ISBN: 978-0-7180-7529-3

Library of Congress Control Number: 2017939647

Printed in the United States of America
23 24 25   PC   10 9 8 7 6 5 4

Mfr: PC / Hagerstown, MD / February 2023 / PO #12192379

*To all dog lovers: no matter where life takes you,
your dog will always be there for you.*

STRETCH!

The little dog stretched her legs and sighed. It was hard to live all alone in the blazing hot Gobi Desert.

Maybe today I'll find a friend, she thought hopefully.

Just then a strange noise in the distance made her ears perk up. *I'm going to chase that noise*, the curious dog decided.

She took off, racing across the sandy dunes.

S T R E T C H !

A man named Dion stretched his strong leg muscles and checked his supplies one last time. He and hundreds of others were getting ready to run a race across the Gobi Desert that took seven days to complete. He had trained long and hard and was ready to go.

POP!

The starting gun fired.
Dion took off, racing across the sandy dunes.

THUMP-THUMP-THUMP-THUMP-THUMP!

The ground shook beneath the dog. And then she saw the most amazing sight—friends! So many friends. And they were even playing chase!

The wind blew back her ears, and her paws sent sand flying behind her. She was going to catch them!

Dion focused on the trail ahead as he ran. "Always look forward," he said to himself. "Never look back."

That's what he told himself every race. That's what he needed to do to win.

He looked down and to his surprise, there was a little dog running beside him.

"RUFF-RUFF!"

The dog barked and gave him a doggy smile. She liked the sound of his voice. This was the best game of chase she had ever played!

Could this man be my friend? She kept running beside him.

The temperature was 120 degrees, and Dion was so thirsty! He gulped down some water, and it trickled down his chin and splashed onto his shirt.

"You must be thirsty too!" He knelt beside the panting pup and poured water into his cupped hand. She was thirsty too!

The racers kept running—through the sandy dunes, up the rocky slopes, under the burning sun. The dog's legs were short, but she ran fast to keep up with Dion.

"I THINK I'LL CALL YOU GOBI,"

Dion said to her, "because you are as tough as the Gobi Desert!"

"Yip-yip!" Gobi barked in agreement. She ran ahead, then circled back to her friend, barking playfully as she encouraged him too.

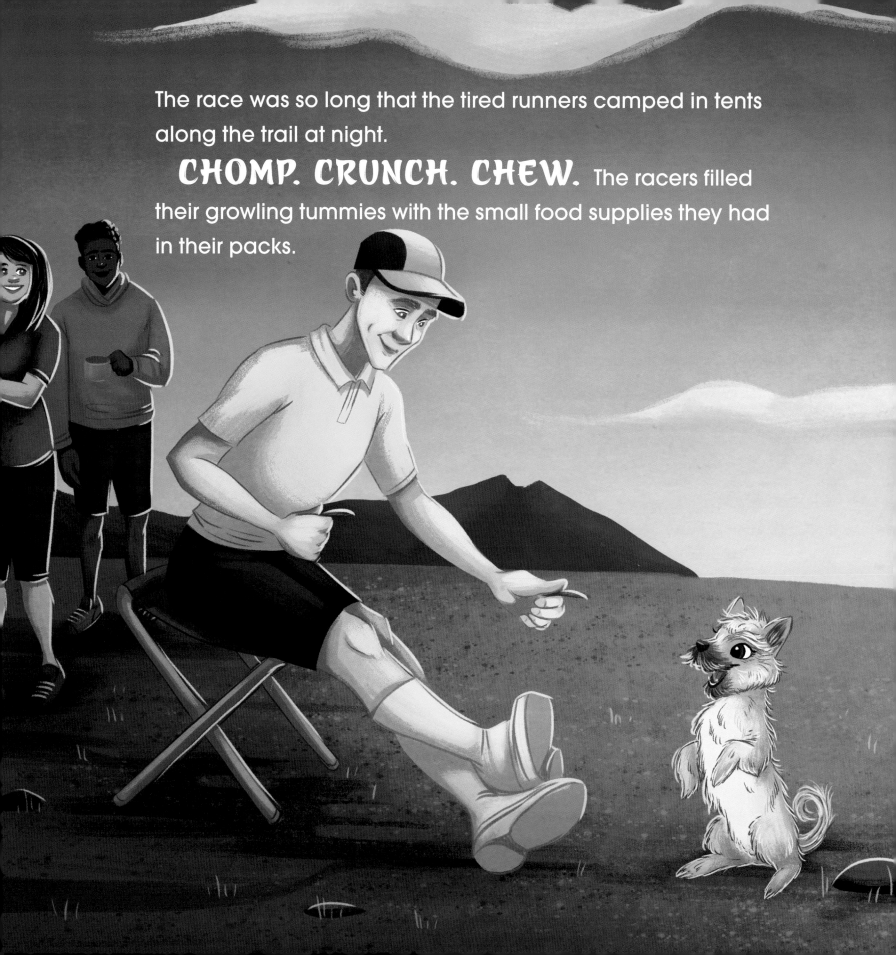

The race was so long that the tired runners camped in tents along the trail at night.

CHOMP. CRUNCH. CHEW. The racers filled their growling tummies with the small food supplies they had in their packs.

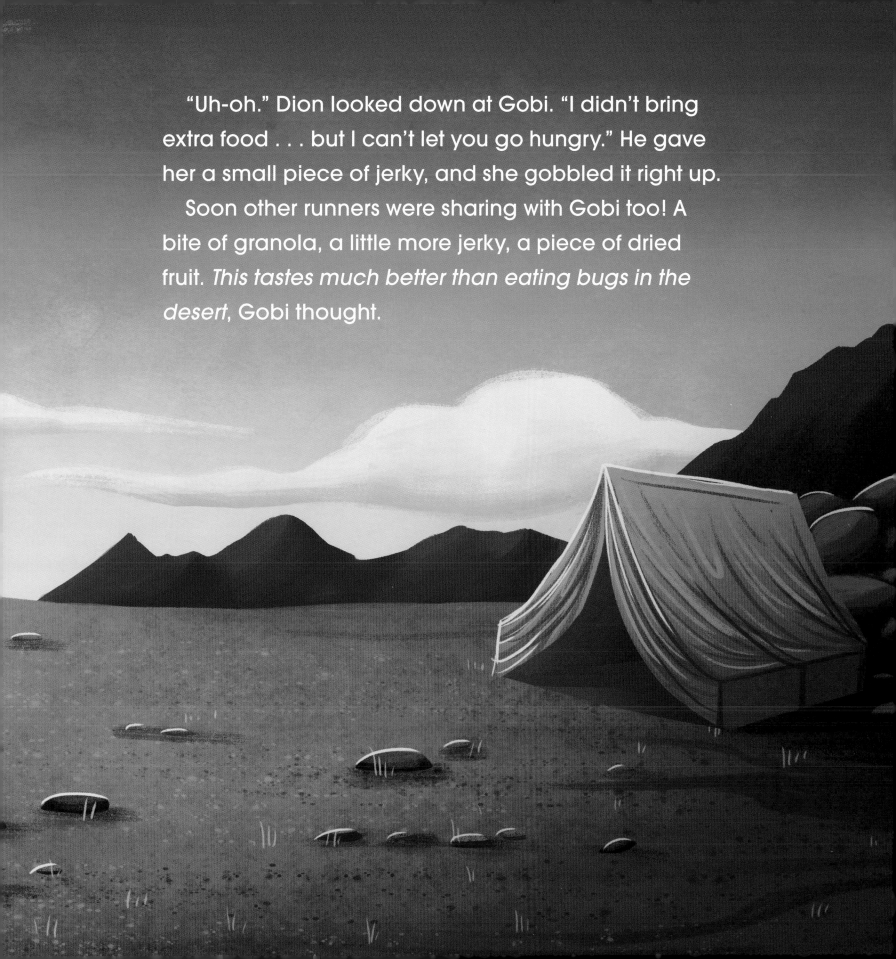

"Uh-oh." Dion looked down at Gobi. "I didn't bring extra food . . . but I can't let you go hungry." He gave her a small piece of jerky, and she gobbled it right up.

Soon other runners were sharing with Gobi too! A bite of granola, a little more jerky, a piece of dried fruit. *This tastes much better than eating bugs in the desert*, Gobi thought.

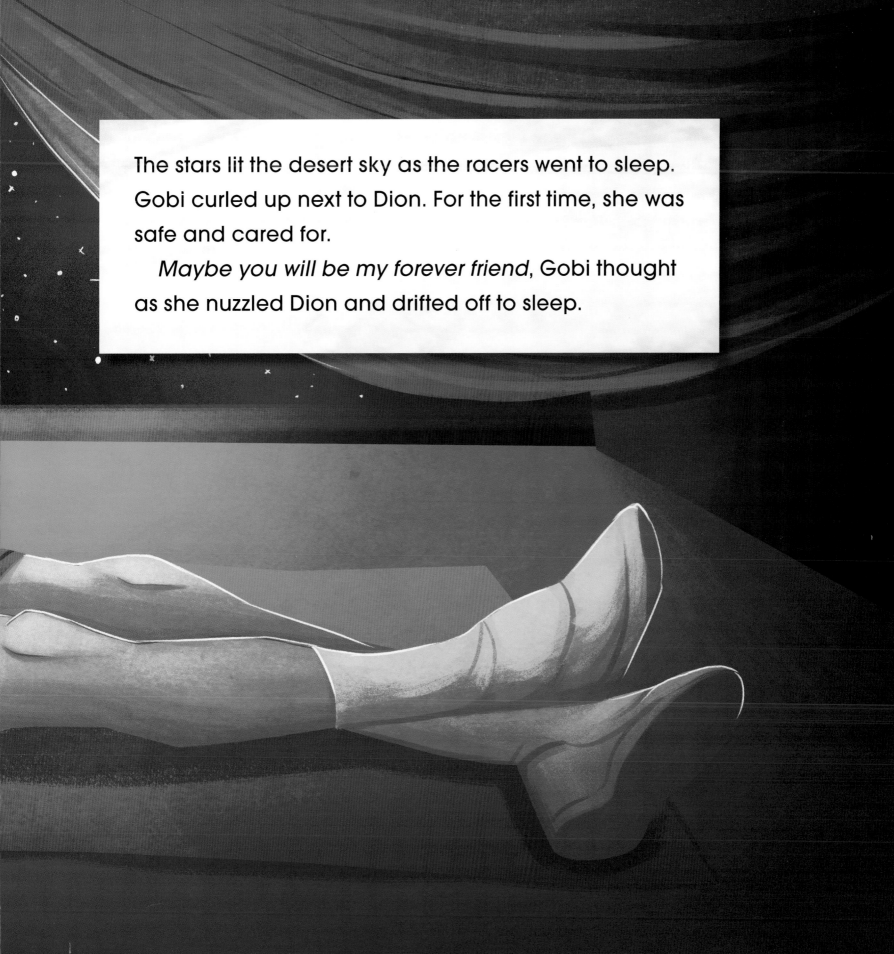

The stars lit the desert sky as the racers went to sleep. Gobi curled up next to Dion. For the first time, she was safe and cared for.

Maybe you will be my forever friend, Gobi thought as she nuzzled Dion and drifted off to sleep.

The two friends continued racing together. One day the course went through a rushing river. Dion ran into the waist-deep water as it splashed and pushed against him.

"Arf, arf!" Gobi whimpered from the shore. *Oh, no*, she thought. *My friend is leaving. And the water is too deep and rough for me.*

"WOOF, WOOF!" PLEASE COME BACK!

Big puppy tears filled her eyes. Dion was almost gone.

"Oh, no. Where's Gobi?" Dion asked himself, realizing she was not with him.

He broke his own rule and looked back to see Gobi pacing the shore and barking for him. He had a hard decision to make. He could keep going to win the race, or he could go back to get his friend.

"I'm coming, Gobi!" He rushed back to shore and scooped her up in his arms. "We're a team," Dion told Gobi.

"I WON'T LEAVE YOU BEHIND!"

Gobi knew she had found her forever friend.

Days went by, and they ran side by side. They were so tired, hungry, and sore. When Gobi was tired, Dion carried her. And when Dion was tired, she barked her happy bark and wagged her tail to encourage him.

"I see it, Gobi! I see the finish line!" The blazing sun made it sparkle in the distance.

Closer, closer, closer.

They crossed the finish line together, and the people cheered wildly!

Dion and Gobi each received a shiny medal. They knew they earned more than medals, though. They had each earned a friend for life.

AUTHOR'S NOTE

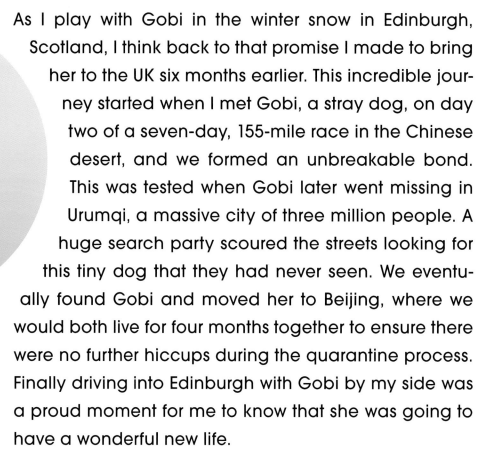

As I play with Gobi in the winter snow in Edinburgh, Scotland, I think back to that promise I made to bring her to the UK six months earlier. This incredible journey started when I met Gobi, a stray dog, on day two of a seven-day, 155-mile race in the Chinese desert, and we formed an unbreakable bond. This was tested when Gobi later went missing in Urumqi, a massive city of three million people. A huge search party scoured the streets looking for this tiny dog that they had never seen. We eventually found Gobi and moved her to Beijing, where we would both live for four months together to ensure there were no further hiccups during the quarantine process. Finally driving into Edinburgh with Gobi by my side was a proud moment for me to know that she was going to have a wonderful new life.

Of course, there was still one final hurdle to jump, and that was Lara, my cat. My wife, Lucja, and I were nervous as we introduced them. At that first meeting between the two, Gobi watched me as I petted Lara, showing Lara the same love and care I show her. This must have been when Gobi realized Lara was now her friend too. Watching them now chasing a tennis ball together in the lounge room or sleeping next to each other, it's amazing to see how much they already love each other.

Gobi's life has changed forever. Mine too, but I wouldn't change a thing. I found my Gobi.